THE S   R   Y

The Planets

Patrick Moore

Illustrated by Paul Doherty

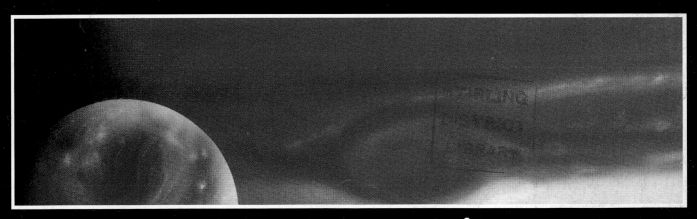

Riverswift

London

First published 1994

1 3 5 7 9 10 8 6 4 2

Design: David West Children's Book Design

This edition published in the United Kingdom in 1996 by
Riverswift, Random House, 20 Vauxhall Bridge Road, London SW1V 2SA

Illustrations by Paul Doherty
Additional illustrations by Mike Lacey and Ian Thompson
Photocredits: Pages16 and 72: Science Photo Library; page 28: Melies
(Courtesy Kobal Collection); page 32: Frank Spooner Pictures; pages 36 and
37: Roger Vlitos

Random House Australia (Pty) Limited, 20 Alfred Street, Milsons Point, Sydney,
New South Wales 2061, Australia

Random House New Zealand Limited, 18 Poland Road, Glenfield, Auckland
10, New Zealand

Random House South Africa (Pty) Limited, PO Box 337, Bergvlei, South Africa

Random House UK Limited Reg. No. 954009

A CIP catalogue record of this book is available from the British Library

ISBN 0 099678 9 18

Printed in Hong Kong

*My grateful thanks are due to Paul Doherty for his splendid
pictures, and to Lynn Lockett for all her help and encouragement.*
P.M.

Contents

The solar system

The Earth is what we call a planet, and it moves around the sun, taking one year to go once around. The moon goes around the Earth. It is smaller than the sun, but it looks as big as the sun because it is much closer to us. There are eight other planets also moving around the sun. Some of these planets have moons of their own.

Mercury

Venus

Earth

Mars

Asteroids

The closest planet to the sun is Mercury. Then come Venus, Earth, and Mars, all of which are quite small. Further away than Mars

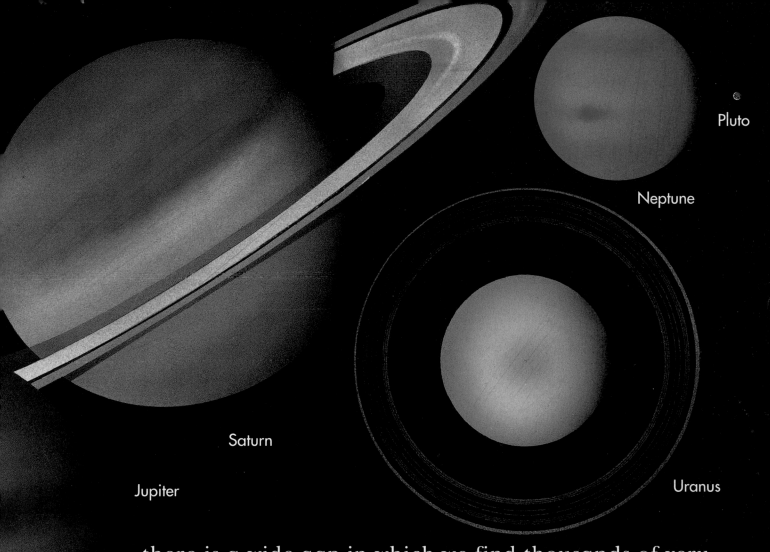

Pluto

Neptune

Saturn

Jupiter

Uranus

there is a wide gap in which we find thousands of very
small worlds which we call minor planets or asteroids.
Beyond come four very big planets, Jupiter, Saturn,
Uranus, and Neptune, with one small planet, Pluto.
Together this whole group is known as the solar system.

Mars in the night sky

<u>Looking at the planets</u>

Like our moon, the planets have no light of their own. We can see them because they are being lit up

by the sun, just as you can light up a ball in a dark room by shining a lamp on it.

The stars are very like the sun, and are very hot, but they seem much less bright than the sun because they are further away. The planets look like stars, but they are really very different, and are much closer than any of the stars. They move slowly around in the sky, and this is how people first found out they are not at all like the stars.

How the planets move

All the planets go around the sun; the closer ones move much more quickly than those which are further away. The Earth takes one year (365 days) to go once around the sun, but Mercury takes only 88 days, while Pluto takes 248 years. If you could live on Pluto, you would have to wait 248 years for your first birthday!

1 Mercury
2 Venus
3 Earth
4 Mars
5 Asteroids
6 Jupiter
7 Saturn
8 Uranus
9 Neptune
10 Pluto

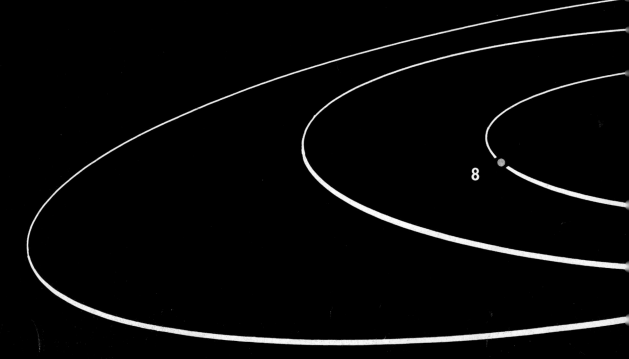

Venus, Mars, Jupiter, and Saturn are so bright that you can find them easily. Mercury always keeps close to the sun. You can just see Uranus but the two last planets, Neptune and Pluto, are so faint that you cannot see them at all unless you use a telescope.

Going to the planets

Although twelve men so far have been to the moon, nobody has yet been to any of the planets. It would take a very long time to get there. But rockets have been sent past all the planets except Pluto, and have sent back pictures of them, so at least we know what they are like.

I am sure you have seen firework rockets. Rockets of this kind work in the same way as the rockets which have been sent into space, but the space-rockets have to have very powerful rocket motors – otherwise they would not be able to go fast enough to get away from the Earth's gravity.

Saturn V rocket taking off

Mercury

The hot planets The

first two planets,

Mercury and Venus,

are very hot. It is not

easy to see Mercury,

because it always stays

so close to the sun. It is

small, and has no air, so

nobody could live there.

The next planet, Venus, is nearly as big as the Earth. It can be

very bright, and you can often see it in the west after sunset or in

the east before the sun rises. It has very thick air, which we could

not breathe, and it is so hot that any water there would boil away.

It will be a long time before anyone can go to Venus for a visit.

Venus

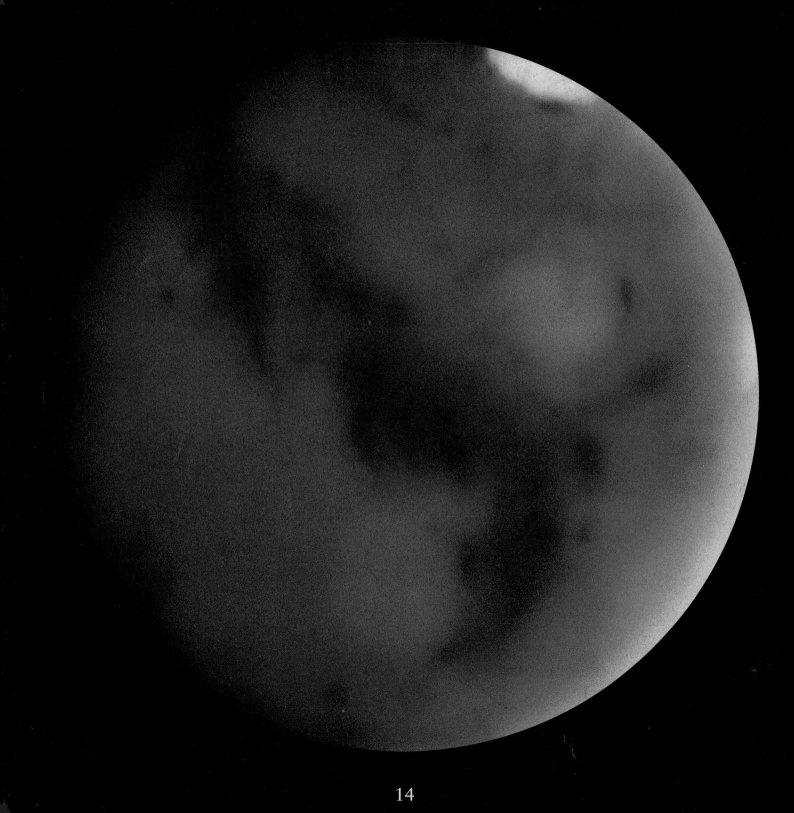

The red planet

The first planet beyond the Earth is Mars. It is very red, and it is smaller than the Earth, though bigger than the moon. By using telescopes, which make far-away things seem closer, we can see that Mars has ice at its poles, just as the Earth has. There are no seas, and it is always

View from the surface of Mars

very cold; the air is so thin that we could not breathe it, and we do not think that there is any life there.

Mars has two moons. Both are very small, and not like our moon. All the same, it would be odd to see two moons in the sky! People may be able to go to Mars before long.

The biggest planet Jupiter

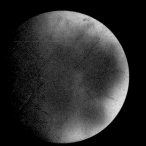

Europa

is the biggest planet, and you can see it well for part of every year; it is much brighter than any of the stars. It takes nearly twelve years to go around the sun, but it has a very short day, less than ten hours long.

Ganymede

Jupiter is not like Earth. Its surface is made up of gas, so we could never land a rocket there.

On it we can see lines which we call

cloud belts. We can also see the

Great Red Spot, which is a huge storm in

Jupiter's gas.

Io

Jupiter has 16 moons, and of these four

are big; one of them, called

Ganymede, is even

bigger than the

planet

Mercury. You

can see these

four moons with

any telescope.

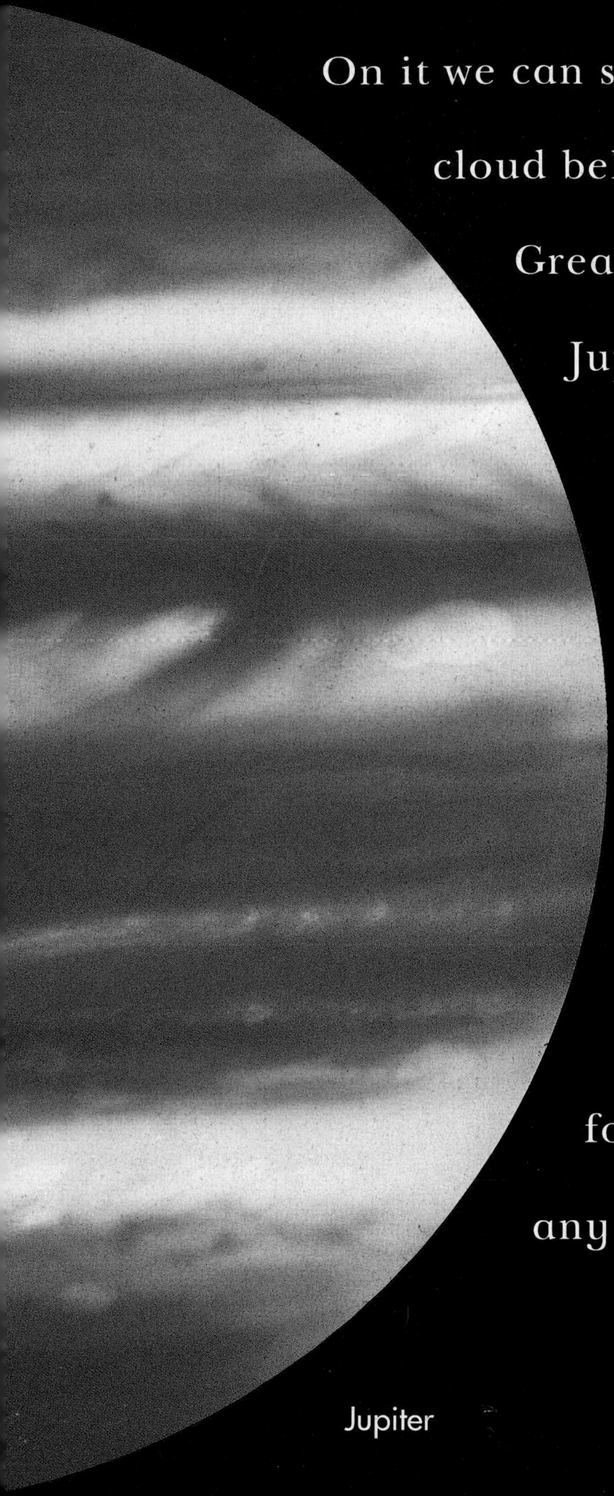

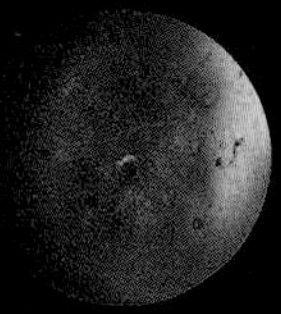

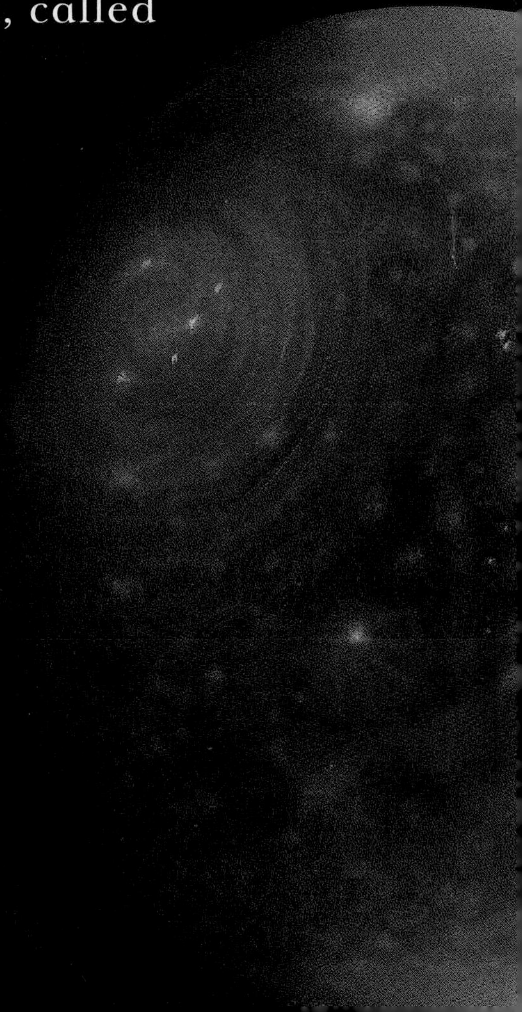

Callisto

Jupiter

The planet with the rings

The next planet is called Saturn. It is smaller than Jupiter, but much bigger than the Earth, and looks like a bright star in the sky.

Like Jupiter, Saturn has a surface made up of gas. It is very beautiful, because it has rings around it, though you cannot see them without a telescope. The rings are made up of little bits of ice moving around Saturn.

Saturn has 18 known moons although astronomers suspect there may be more, at least three, or perhaps even as many as seven.

One of Saturn's moons, Titan, has thick air, and is so cold that we could not live there.

Saturn's rings are made of pieces of ice.

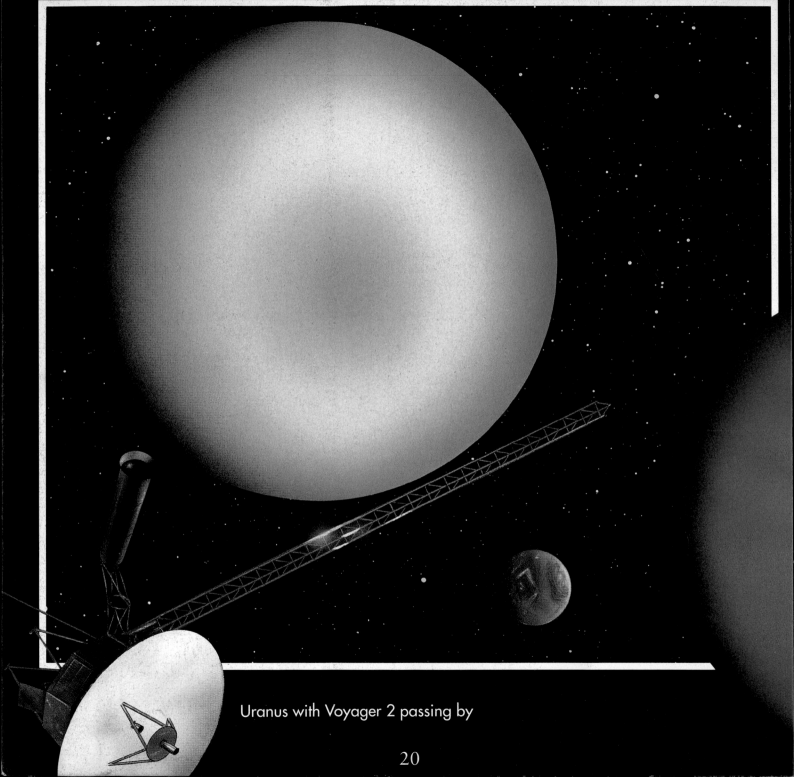

Uranus with Voyager 2 passing by

Very cold planets

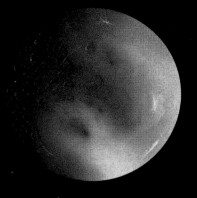

Pluto

The last three planets are so far away that they look faint. Uranus and Neptune are about half as big as Saturn, and both have moons; Uranus has 15 moons, Neptune, 8. Uranus is green, Neptune, blue. A spaceship called Voyager 2 passed by them both, so we have good pictures of them.

Pluto is smaller than our moon, and no spaceship yet can reach it. It is so cold that air of the kind we know would freeze. If you could go to Pluto, the sun would look only like a very bright star.

Now that you know what you are looking for, go outdoors at night and find the closer planets for yourself!

Neptune

The Hubble space telescope can see a very long way into space.

Other Earths?

We could not live on any of the other planets which move around the sun. Some are too hot; others are too cold, and they do not have the right sort of air for us to breathe. But it may well be that other stars have planets of their own, with life on them.

If this is true – and we cannot be sure! – then there may be people like ourselves. We cannot send spaceships to planets of other stars, because they are too far away, but one day we may be able to find out that we are not alone in space.

Whether this happens or not, we may be sure that in the next few years we are going to discover many new and exciting facts about space and our universe.

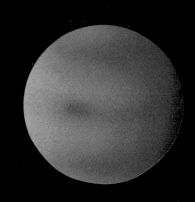

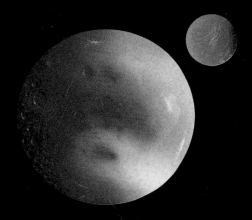

Index

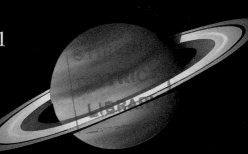